AROUND TOPSHAM
IN OLD PHOTOGRAPHS

AN AERIAL PHOTOGRAPH OF THE SITE OF TOPSHAM which occupies a tongue of land between the Clyst and Exe rivers. The Exeter Canal borders the Exminster marshes, which are criss-crossed by drainage channels as seen in the foreground. (Photograph by Aerofilms Ltd.)

AROUND TOPSHAM
IN OLD PHOTOGRAPHS
COUNTESS WEAR TO LYMPSTONE

COLLECTED BY
BARBARA ENTWISTLE
ROSEMARY BURTON
CATHY MAGUIRE
HAROLD PYM
ANN WHITAKER

ALAN SUTTON

Alan Sutton Publishing Limited
Phoenix Mill · Far Thrupp · Stroud · Gloucestershire

First Published 1990

Copyright © Topsham Museum Society 1990

All rights reserved. No part of this publication may be reproduced, stored in a retrieval system, or transmitted, in any form or by any means, electronic, mechanical, photocopying, recording or otherwise, without the prior permission of the publishers and copyright holders.

British Library Cataloguing in Publication Data

Around Topsham in old photographs : Countess Wear to Lympstone.
1. Devon. Topsham region, history
I. Topsham museum Society
942.356

ISBN 0–86299–717–8

Dedication: to the late Mr Donald Steven

Typeset in 9/10 Korinna.
Typesetting and origination by
Alan Sutton Publishing Limited.
Printed in Great Britain by
Dotesios Printers Limited.

CONTENTS

	INTRODUCTION	6
1.	THE RIVER	9
2.	THE TOWN	57
3.	THE SURROUNDING AREA: COUNTESS WEAR, CLYST ST GEORGE, EBFORD AND EXTON, LYMPSTONE	95
4.	PUBLIC SERVICES	127
5.	EVENTS AND SOCIAL LIFE	135
	ACKNOWLEDGEMENTS	160

FISHERMEN ON THE QUAY.

INTRODUCTION

The photographs in this collection were first assembled for an exhibition held at Topsham Museum in the summer of 1989. The interest taken in this exhibition has led to this publication, which we hope will be a record of an older Topsham which is fast disappearing. The photographs cover the century between 1850 and 1950. They illustrate not only the past life in Topsham but also that of the group of riverside settlements along the Exe from Countess Wear to Lympstone, including nearby farming areas which supplied food and very often manpower to vessels leaving the port of Topsham for overseas or coastal destinations.

The historic port of Topsham stands on the eastern bank of the River Exe, some four miles south-east of Exeter, immediately above the confluence of the Exe with its tributary, the Clyst, and some six miles from the sea. For hundreds of years sailing vessels crossing the bar at Exmouth and entering the River Exe found a wide, sheltered estuary here, with deep pools for safe anchorage, yet easily accessible to the markets of Exeter via the port of Topsham with its attendant facilities. From 1316, when its first stone quay was constructed, Topsham began to prosper, becoming the principal port of Exeter for overseas trade.

By the 1850s the town of Topsham supported a prosperous maritime community of some 3,400 people, a figure which increased to 3,503 by 1861, before falling quite sharply in the 1870s and 1880s. Its prosperity was based on its shipbuilding industry and on its continuing function as a port.

Robert Davy and his son, Daniel Bishop Davy, who had earlier built up a substantial shipbuilding industry, first at Countess Wear, then at Topsham's

Passage Yard, had retired by the 1850s. Countess Wear, no longer a shipbuilding centre, still imported limestone and culm for its kilns and would continue to find work for more than two hundred people at its paper mills for a further thirty-five years. Lympstone's shipbuilding days were now over, and fishing and agriculture had become its principal economic concerns.

John Holman was the key figure in extending Topsham's prosperity into the 1850s and 1860s, as he took over from the Davys their yards and premises, giving continued employment to their skilled workforce. A Master Mariner, shipowner, shipbuilder, and marine insurer, John Holman at this time was at the height of his creativity. By 1850, the firm of John Holman & Sons was in existence, concerned with marine insurance. By 1858 John Holman was building wooden sailing vessels at both his upper and lower yards; his new dry dock was in operation; and at his third yard at Strand End, leased by the Row Brothers, other building work was in progress. But this story of success did not last long after John Holman's death in 1863. His sons stayed in Topsham for a further ten years constructing both wooden and composite sailing vessels, but competition from the railways, the establishment of Exmouth Docks, the increasing size of merchant sailing vessels all contributed to making it uneconomic for the firm to continue in Topsham and the Insurance Department moved to London on 3 October 1873.

Yet, from this time until the 1930s, Topsham-owned sailing vessels continued to find work; some still trading overseas, most engaging in coastal trades or fishing. Many Topsham families owned a few small sailing vessels, which were later fitted with engines. By the 1920s and '30s, however, such vessels were increasingly expensive to maintain and some were pushed into the banks and abandoned. Motor fishing vessels were once again built in Topsham during the Second World War, and boats for the leisure market continue to be built today.

Topsham had enjoyed an earlier period of great prosperity in the late seventeenth and early eighteenth centuries, when great quantities of Devonshire-made serge cloth were exported overseas from Topsham Quay, principally to Holland. The wealth which accrued to Topsham from this trade led to more general affluence, and to the building of the Strand houses with their Dutch-style gables, but also to many religious, and educational initiatives.

The Puritan influence was strong in Topsham in the seventeenth century as in most other ports. The influential Revd Amos Short lived in Topsham between 1645 and 1650, and a strong Presbyterian group held meetings here before their chapel was closed down under the Act of Uniformity. The Society of Friends also found strong support in Topsham at an early date, encouraged by the visit made by Mr George Fox in 1655.

Topsham has had no single benefactor, but many prosperous merchants and shipowners have benefited the town. George Hodder, for example, a merchant shipowner who engaged in the Dutch trade, is credited with building a new Presbyterian chapel in today's Victoria Road — a chapel which in its heyday in the 1720s attracted some six hundred supporters. A bequest by the shipmaster, Sam Elliott, a Presbyterian who died in 1768, gave funds for the education of poor children and this led to the setting up of Elliott's School in a room near the chapel.

At a later date the shipbuilder John Holman bequeathed funds to build the Methodist church in Fore Street. His grandson, Herbert Holman, gave land by the river for a children's recreation ground. Miss Dorothy Holman more recently left her property at No. 25 the Strand for use as a museum.

The earliest school in the neighbourhood was the Lady Seward School in Clyst St George, a Church of England school which was established as early as 1704. One interesting subject taught to pupils as part of the curriculum was navigation. National Schools were in existence in Topsham by 1833, with Revd H. Thorp, the incumbent of St Margaret's church, their treasurer.

To help poor children find apprenticeships, Mrs Ann Collier, a prominent member of the Society of Friends, bequeathed £500 in three per cent consols in 1777. This and other bequests are today carefully administered by the Topsham Market House Trust and used for the benefit of Topsham people.

It is against this background that these photographs may be a useful record of some of the continuing activities of this close-knit, self-reliant community, international in its outlook, earning its living from the sea.

SECTION ONE
The River

TOPSHAM QUAY FROM THE AIR BEFORE 1925. A railway spur from the station was extended down to the quay in 1861. Ropes were stretched across Fore Street Hill and Quay Hill for safety when trains were about to arrive. The line was taken up in 1963. Since then a road has been built from the station to the quay called Holman Way, which is still crossed by the old railway footbridge.

TWO MEN ON THE EDGE OF THE QUAY, standing on a later extension to the original quay built in 1316 by Hugh Courtenay, later Earl of Devon, who sought to encourage trade to Topsham. In 1861 the London and South Western Railway Company greatly enlarged the old quay by extending it further out into the river and by including the former Steamer Quay and some small coal yards within the overall quay area.

THE KING'S WEIGH BEAM stands in front of the old Quaymaster's house and workshop on the town quay. The weigh beam is representative of a whole range of services once available to vessels at the quay — anchorage, wharfage, weighage, cranage, cellarage — for which dues were charged. In 1769 the quay was purchased by the Exeter Chamber. For many years the custom-house was at No. 48 Fore Street (the present W.A. Nott's grocery shop).

MR DANIEL TROUT, was Quaymaster of Topsham until his retirement, following in this office both his father, Mr William Trout, and his grandfather, Mr Daniel Charles Trout. Mr D.C. Trout founded the boatbuilding firm of Trout & Son in 1902. The family business still flourishes, continuing its fine tradition in the building of and repairs to wooden and clinker-built vessels.

TOPSHAM.

To be Let,

BY AUCTION,

AT THE GLOBE INN, TOPSHAM,

On WEDNESDAY, the 24th day of SEPTEMBER inst.,

AT FIVE O'CLOCK IN THE AFTERNOON PRECISELY,

FOR THE TERM OF ONE YEAR FROM MICHAELMAS, 1851,

Subject to such conditions as shall then be produced, THE

TOWN DUES, QUAY DUES AND CELLARAGE,

INCLUDING THE

DUES ON FOREIGN GOODS AND COALS,

ARISING AT TOPSHAM AFORESAID,

BELONGING TO THE COUNCIL OF EXETER,

TOGETHER WITH THE WHARFINGER'S

DWELLING HOUSE,

OFFICES AND CELLARS.

For further Particulars, application must be made to

Mr. GIDLEY,

TOWN CLERK, EXETER.

Exeter, 10th September, 1851.

TREWMAN AND CO., PRINTERS, EXETER.

A NOTICE PUBLISHED IN 1851. An invitation to bid for the right to collect the dues of the port of Topsham.

STEAM PACKETS FROM STEAMER QUAY. A regular service to London from Topsham was operated from the early 1830s by the St George Steam Packet Company, with vessels such as the *William* and the *Superb* carrying passengers, goods and even livestock. The steam packets moored up to the Steamer Quay, south of the original, small, Town Quay. The *Zephyr*, advertised above, was an improved type of steamer which operated until at least 1844. By this time the fare for travel to London on deck had risen to 10s. with the cabin fare £1 1s. In the 1840s steamship services were on offer to France and the Channel Islands as well as to London. The Steam Packet Inn near the quay commemorates these days.

TOPPINGS WHARF,
SOUTHWARK, S.E.

THE FOLLOWING
CONSTANT TRADERS

Lie SIX WORKING DAYS each at the above Wharf, to take in goods for the undermentioned places:—

TO BE DELIVERED AT
TOPSHAM & EXETER,

Truscott, Son, & Simmons, Typ.

The act of God, the Queen's enemies, and all the dangers and accidents of the seas and navigation, of whatever nature or kind soever (not happening through the default of the masters or mariners) excepted. The Owners or Masters will not be accountable for leakage, wastage, nor loss by vermin, nor loss occasioned by imperfect directions, marks, or packing, nor for goods after they are landed at the places of delivery.

DEVON	E. Broom	FAME	T. Stockham
THAMES	T. E. Trickey	GROCER	R. H. Norman
UNION	G. Gibbs		

The DEVON, E. BROOM, Master,
IS NOW LOADING FOR
EXETER & TOPSHAM,

Vessels load for Chester, Truro,   *Exeter, and Weymouth.*

Alphington	Budleigh	Exmouth	Oakhampton	Taunton
Ashburton	Crediton	Holdsworthy	Runnington	Torrington
Barnstaple	Chudleigh	Honiton	Salterton	Topsham
Bideford	Chumleigh	Ipplepen	Sandford	Teignmouth
Bovey-Tracey	Crockernwell	Kingsteignton	Silverton	Thorverton
Barkhamer	Colyton	Kingsnympton	Star-Cross	Torr-abbey
Bradninch	Collumpton	Kenton	Southmoulton	Wellington
Bridgewater	Dawlish	Lympstone	Sidmouth	Wiveliscombe
Buckland	Dulverton	Morton Hampstead	St. Mary Ottery	Wilstone
Broadclist	Exeter	orth Tawton	Tiverton	and all places adjacent

The conditions on which goods are collected or received at this Wharf, are as follows, viz.:—the Wharfingers will not be accountable or engage to forward goods by any particular vessel, though named in the receipt given or in any order, or named in the bills as loading, neither for loss or damage by fire, vermin, high tides or other water, either at this wharf, or other wharf, dock, or warehouse, where goods may be lying for collection, by cart or lighter, nor for any delay in sending for such goods, nor for breakage, leakage, or wastage, act of God, the Queen's enemies, dangers or accidents of the sea, rivers or navigation, of whatsoever nature or kind, or loss occasioned by imperfect marks or directions (that is where goods are not marked with the name and address at full length), nor by imperfect packing; neither will any advice be given of the shipment of goods which may have been left out of any former vessel or vessels. All goods will be subject to a general lien for any previous balance due from the parties to whom they belong. All goods received by water carriage will be subject to the usual charge for wharfage. Please to send the particulars of what the packages contain, and money for wharf charges. Shippers are particularly requested not to advise their correspondents till the goods are actually shipped; and are also recommended to insure by "ship or ships," and not by any particular vessel named in the receipt given. The receipt given will be in force only six months.

N.B.—Shippers are apprised that Goods sent to any other than the above Wharf for Shipment in this Vessel, will not be received without payment of Half Wharfage.

The Last Day of taking in Goods is Thursday   186

J. H. & G. SCOVELL, Wharfingers.
PETER PALMER, Agent, Exeter.

Date	Wharfage, &c. Packages....	£.	s.	d.	Received.

CONSTANT TRADERS. Regular services from London to the River Exe for the delivery of goods to most parts of Devon continued well into the 1860s, as is shown on the bill above. All the vessels named here, mostly schooners, were built in Topsham, in Thomas Bowden's yard in the 1820s.

THE VENTURER PILOT BOAT, *E1*, at Exmouth Dock in front of a four-masted schooner and a steamer with a 'woodbine' funnel. From 1687 'all masters of ships or barks drawing more than 5 ft of water' were to take a pilot: 'the rule and charges to be hung up in a frame at Topsham'. In 1878 six river-pilots were stationed here. More recently Trinity House pilots worked from Exmouth. The pilots knew the dangers, and the safe navigable channel from the Fairway Buoy to Turf Lock and to Topsham Quay.

A FAMILY OF RIVER PILOTS. Four generations of the Pym family of Topsham are shown here: Mr Edwin Pitfield Pym (1846–1937), who served before the mast in square-riggers travelling round the world before returning to Topsham to work as a river pilot for the next thirty-five years; Mr Pym's son, Mr Edgar (Bruce) Pym; his grandson, Edgar, and his great-grandson, also Edgar. Mr Bruce Pym's daughter married Mr Percy Bradford, another Trinity House pilot, who retired in 1965 after eighteen years service. Below: Mr Edwin Pym with two of his friends.

PILOT BOAT *THE QUINTET*, so-called because five pilots used her. In 1932 the five pilots were Mr Percy Bradford, Mr Reg Pym, Mr Ern Knight, Mr Edgar (Bruce) Pym and Mr Fred Knight (pictured below). They piloted vessels, such as the tanker *Ben Johnson*, to Topsham or up the canal to Exeter.

PASSAGE OR FERRY. A member of the Bolt family at the slipway on the Exminster side of the river. Exeter City Council took over the ferry in 1966 from St Thomas Rural District Council, who had acquired it from Heavitree Brewery in 1943. A deed dated 1736 refers to a licence given to Benjamin Buttall and John Wear (owners of the passage boat from Topsham to Exminster) by the lord of the manor of Exminster, to make a passage of a breadth of twelve feet, 'fitt for man and horse' over 'all that part of a certain salt marsh called Newlands ... for the new landing place of the passengers on the said marsh'.

MR ROBERT BOLT in 1934, when he was eighty-four years old and still active as a ferryman, seen here with his son, Ben, and his granddaughter, Nancy. Mr Robert Bolt and his wife kept the Passage Inn. (See page 21.)

THE FERRY. Two young girls, carrying their belongings in small wicker baskets, are returning from Exminster by ferry. Many young people used to work in Exminster, often at the hospital there. The ferry was an essential means of transport to work as recently as 1930, when Mrs Dean (then Kathleen Collacott) used it daily for six years to travel to her teaching post at Cockwood School. Her journey started at 7.30 a.m., when she left Rose Cott, Ebford, and cycled to the Passage Inn. From here Mr Ben Bolt would row her across the river for 2d. She would then walk across the marshes to Exminster station and catch the train to Starcross, from where she would walk to Cockwood, arriving at school at 8.50 a.m. Below: The ferry at low tide, c. 1900.

THE PASSAGE INN. The above, earlier view is from c. 1900, when Mr and Mrs Robert Bolt lived at the inn. To the left is an advertisement from the time when George C. Leach was the licensee.

MR AND MRS ROBERT BOLT of the Passage Inn with their family. (Photograph courtesy of Miss N. Burgess.)

OUTSIDE THE NEW ENTRANCE TO THE PASSAGE INN. A fine salmon, more than 33 lbs in weight, is held by Mr Bill Newman, Mr Harry Pym, Mr Denzil Pym and Mr George Leach, landlord of the Passage Inn. It was Mr Leach who extended the inn to these premises next door.

DAVYS' PASSAGE YARD: HOLMANS' UPPER YARD. Robert Davy of Countess Wear bought land at Passage in 1803/4 and these premises 'he enlarged by extending them towards low water, forming slipways, etc. for the purpose of building and repairing ships'. From this site Mr Davy launched warships for the navy and built many merchant vessels. In 1826 Mr Daniel Bishop Davy took over his father's shipbuilding business at Passage and continued the work there. On the left is the site of the Davys' warehouse, which was rebuilt by John Holman in 1850 and used as a sail loft. The pier was part of the property of the Follett family, who imported timber.

SHIPMASTER FOR THE DAVYS. Captain John Sully (1805–92), master mariner, worked for the Davys for many years as Master of the *Darby Allen*, a sailing barge of 77 tons, built in 1833 by Mr Robert Davy at Countess Wear. The *Darby Allen* was reportedly 'swamped in 1841' but her crew was saved. The vessel continued trading until 1861. By 1857, Captain Sully was a shipowner himself: part owner of the *Friendship*, a ketch built by John Holman & Sons.

LAUNCHING THE *MYTH* in 1856. A schooner of 97 tons, built at the Holmans' upper yard, the *Myth* is shown here in this painting rigged and flying the Holman house flag.

THE FIGUREHEAD OF THE *CENTURION* is attached to the riverside corner of the former sail loft, part of the shipbuilding complex of the Holmans' upper yard. HMS *Centurion* was launched at Pembroke on 2 May 1844, an 80-ton ship. She was broken up in 1870. Her connection with Topsham has not been established. Another figurehead, nicknamed 'Angus' may be seen in the Topsham Museum.

FOLLETT LODGE, as depicted in a charming nineteenth-century painting (above) and, when photographed in the early 1900s (below). John Follett of Sidmouth (1701–86) first moved to Topsham in the 1740s and acquired land at Passage. His son, Benjamin (1736–1803) and his grandson, also Benjamin (1762–1833), were timber merchants and shipowners, with business interests in Newfoundland. The saltmarsh area north of the old dock served as their timber pound. The family owned sawmills and the former ropewalk in today's Victoria Road. William Webb Follett, who became MP for Exeter (1837–45) and Attorney-General in Peel's administration (1845), was born here. The property was much altered in the 1920s.

ELEANOR'S BOWER, an attractive summer-house, built in the garden above Follett Lodge, with beautiful views across the River Exe. This photograph shows a building with just one room downstairs and one room upstairs. The only access was via this outer stairway. The house was thatched until 1917, when the roof was repaired and covered with Delabole slates taken from the Old Vicarage, which was demolished at this time. The name almost certainly refers to Eleanor Mary Haswell Holman (1837–1917) – on the right – who married Richard Holman, one of John Holman's sons, in 1858. Below: an artist's impression of Eleanor's Bower.

CAPTAIN RICHARD BAGWELL (1784–1856). A remarkable photograph of an old shipmaster, here surrounded by his family, which was taken in 1855 on the veranda of Grove House, Topsham. The young man who has his arm on Captain Bagwell's shoulder is Mr John Holman, jnr. The original photograph from a glass negative is tucked inside the front cover of a log-book which belonged to Captain Bagwell, discovered in 1898 in an old chest at Topsham Dock, but which is now in Devon Record Office. Captain Bagwell had an adventurous life, at one time serving in a whaling ship *The Brothers* in the South Atlantic, at another time ferrying troops to Spain in the *Fanny* during the Napoleonic Wars. (Photograph courtesy of the DRO.)

JOHN BAGWELL HOLMAN (1800–63). The outstanding figure in mid-nineteenth-century Topsham, John Holman was largely responsible for the town's continuing prosperity. Going to sea at the age of twelve with his father, John Holman had more than twenty-five years of practical experience before concentrating on business affairs. He became Lloyds' Surveyor for Topsham in 1839 and held this post until he died. During the 1850s and early '60s he owned three shipbuilding yards in Topsham: Mr D.B. Davy's former Passage Yard, the Lower Yard on the Strand and the Strand End Yard, which was let to the Row Brothers. A public-spirited, religious man, Mr Holman contributed generously to the building of the new Methodist church in Fore street.

GROVE HOUSE – BOARDROOM AND OFFICES. The house stands on the corner of Fore Street and Station Road, and was the home of Mr John Holman and his family as well as being a place of work. The offices of John Holman & Sons were in the single-storey building on the left of the photograph. Board meetings were held in a room added on to the house, on the right, at the top of the outside staircase. John Holman was a pioneer in establishing mutual associations for shipowners. The West of England Marine Insurance Association, founded in 1832, is the 'parent' of the modern 'P & I Clubs' which have spread to many parts of the world and are known as 'Western Clubs'. The Exeter Shipping Insurance Association followed in 1838, with John Holman as secretary, and by 1843 the Association was insuring sixty-two vessels registered in local ports. (Photography courtesy of Devon Library Services.)

JOHN HOLMAN'S PATENT RUDDER. Mr John Holman wrote in 1859 that, 'All practical men engaged in the building or navigation of ships know that one of their great safety valves is the security of the rudder.' He himself had suffered from two ships breaking their rudders, and he was able to produce an improved pintleless rudder which could be unshipped for repairs even at sea. Here the *Courtenay*, a brig of 198 tons, built by John Holman & Sons in 1867, carries the improved rudder. A similar rudder is a rare exhibit in the sail loft at the Topsham Museum.

HOLMAN'S DRY DOCK in a derelict state, c. 1907.

ENGLAND'S ROSE IN TOPSHAM'S DRY DOCK. Built by John Holman & Sons in 1858, *England's Rose*, a barquentine, was the first vessel to use the new dry dock. This attractive photograph is of a painting of her launching by Mr J.B. Goodrich of Topsham. The vessel is depicted high in the dock and looks somewhat unstable but the scene shows a happy occasion when all who worked on her could join in the celebration. Mr Goodrich's sister, Agatha, married Mr William Williams, a fellow artist, in 1850 and together they formed the nucleus of an artists' colony in Topsham. The Williams family lived at North View, the Strand, and their son, Roscoe, also an artist, lived here until his death in 1935.

WORKING PREMISES, such as the sail loft, with a schooner lying alongside in this photograph, c. 1870, occupied most of the riverside area until recently. Such buildings have been converted over the years into attractive houses.

THOMAS HOLMAN (1824–62), master mariner, shipowner, and sailmaker, was one of the five sons of John Holman. He married Miss Mary Nicks on Christmas Day 1854 and came to live at No. 25 the Strand, where, in 1858, he built a sail loft, attached to the back of his house. He was said to be 'very particular about his sails'. This extended building now houses Topsham Museum. This miniature of Thomas Holman was painted in 1855 by Frederick Harding.

A 131 tons	Barque ELIZABETH 377 tons	Barque GENERAL CHASSE 648 tons	Barque RECOVERY 317 t
PTON 218 tons	Schooner FRIENDSHIP	Schooner MYTH Built 1850 97 tons	Ketch OLD TIFF 39 tons
AND'S ROSE Built 1858	Schooner COME ON 198 tons	Brigantine MARSALA 178 tons	Cutter NINA

Painted by Edward Hexter of Teignmouth, 1858

FLEET OF JOHN HOLMAN, sen. This photograph of Edward Hexter's painting of 1858 shows the scale of the achievement of John Holman. Such a fleet was capable of generating profitable trade, visiting all parts of the world.

THE *MARY ANN HOLMAN*, a barque of 272 tons, was built in 1859 by the Holmans for their own use. The vessel traded frequently to South America. Captain Harry Holman (1847–1927) was Master of the *Mary Ann Holman* from 1869 to 1879. The barque was named after Mrs Mary Ann Symons Holman, Mr John Holman's wife. A companion barque was built by the Holmans in 1864, the year after John Holman's death, and named in his honour.

THE BARQUE *HUGH FORTESCUE*, of 505 tons, was built by John Holman & Sons in 1865 for the China trade. Here the vessel is shown after her sale to Norway in 1887, flying the Norwegian flag. (Photograph from the Arendal Museum, Norway.)

CAPTAIN WILLIAM THOMAS HOLMAN (1850–1932), master mariner. Captain Holman was Master of the *Hugh Fortescue* for some years, and also of the *Mary Ann Holman*.

THE *SAM HANFORD* was a sister ship to the *City of Exeter*, both vessels of over 1,000 tons and both sail-assisted steamships. In the 1870s the Holmans bought a fleet of such steamships. The oil painting of the *Sam Hanford*, flying the Holman house flag, is on display at Topsham Museum, on loan from Teignmouth Museum.

CAPTAIN PHILIP HENRY SYMONS WITH HIS FAMILY. Captain Symons was Master of the *City of Exeter* in 1879. His son, Philip Henry, jun., followed in his father's footsteps and, in later years, became master of the SS *Voltaire* and then of her sister ship SS *Vandyke*. This photograph was donated by Mrs Violet Johnson, daughter of Mr Richard Symons, the elder son of Captain Symons, who is shown here on the left as a child. Captain Symons, sen. is buried at Halifax, Canada.

CAPTAIN JAMES PALMER BROWN, Master and part-owner of the *Enmore* steamer of 1,122 tons, built in Stockton in 1872 for John Holman & Sons. Captain Brown's last voyage in his vessel was to New Orleans in 1873, where he loaded cotton for his return journey to 'Havre'. Sadly, he died there of yellow fever at the early age of thirty-three. An account of Captain Brown's last days, including the poignant letter which, apparently in good health, he wrote to his wife three days before his death, may be seen in Topsham Museum.

CAPTAIN CHARLES SCOT SALISBURY, a master mariner engaged in overseas trade, and owner of the schooner *Venus*, of 127 tons, built in Topsham in 1849.

THE *CHARLOTTE* AT CHRISTCHURCH. This Holman-built sailing barge with lee-boards was chiefly used to carry coal from Portsmouth to Christchurch — as much as a thousand tons annually over many years.

'UNCLE' PERIAM. Captain Gilbert Periam married Catherine Holman in 1828 and was known as 'Uncle' Periam by members of the Holman family. A master mariner and shipowner, Captain Periam held part-shares in many Topsham vessels. Captain F.R. Holman tells how there was an old Topsham custom that all colliers were discharged by their crews. After unloading every hundred baskets, the crew could stop work for a pint of beer each, put up by the shipowner. Capt. Periam went further. His crew were invited to his house in Monmouth Street and provided with a good hot dinner, with the captain carving the joint himself. Capt. Holman commented that these were called 'the bad old days'.

CAUTION.

Whereas I did on the 30th day of January last, Assault Mr. FREDERICK WILLIAMS, the Son of the Wharfinger at Topsham, while engaged in his duty, for which the Mayor and Council of Exeter, the Lords of the Quay and Port, have commenced a Prosecution against me, which Prosecution they have consented to forego upon my signing this Acknowledgment, paying the Expenses incurred, and also paying a Fine of Forty Shillings to a Public Charity. Now I do hereby acknowledge my error in committing the said Assault, and promise not to offend again in like manner.

Dated the Fifteenth day of April, 1839.

G. PERIAM.

WITNESS,
JOHN GIDLEY,
TOWN CLERK.

R. J. Trewman, Printer, Exeter.

A PUBLIC APOLOGY. Mr Gilbert Periam, as a young man, makes restitution for his offence. An idea worth trying?

SCHOONERS AT THE QUAY, C. 1900. A three-masted topsail schooner at the Quay and a two-masted topsail schooner further out in the river. The working premises of the Holmans' lower yard are marked by the chimney. Below: A three-masted topsail schooner lying in front of the Quay with a second schooner in the Cut.

ODAMS' MANURE AND CHEMICAL FACTORY. Messrs Phillips took extensive premises at Ebford in 1850 for the manufacture of manures adapted for different crops. By 1886 'Odams' Manure and Chemical Factory occupied the site. Many people still remember when guano was imported from South America in blue-sea ocean-goers, upwards of 250 tons, which used to anchor in the Bight. Dumb barges came down from Topsham to unload the guano in mid-river. A vessel could be emptied in three days but it was a cold, dirty and expensive business. Up to 1,250 tons were brought in during any one month. Barges would be poled up the Clyst river at nearly high tide to be unloaded at Odams' Wharf. After 1861 vessels which came alongside the Quay were off-loaded into railway wagons which were carried right into the factory grounds. The fertilizer was weighed, sorted and bagged and then despatched by railway. Later, various chemicals were mixed and packed for farmers. Written along the side of the building in the photograph is 'Odams Manures Sheep Dips Cattle Wash and Disinfectants'.

THE WORKFORCE in the 1920s. Odams was put up for sale in 1939. The tall chimney came down in 1940.

DANIEL KINSLOW NORTON (1836–1921). Mr D.K. Norton was a successful coal merchant who, in the early 1900s, owned several Brixham-built trawlers which he used in the coal trade, such as the *Rescue*, of 45 tons, built in 1886. She later became a hulk, and is now buried beneath the extension to Trouts' Boatyard. Mr Norton, a religious man, was a well-known lay preacher.

CHEVROLET DELIVERY LORRY. Mr Jim Norton with his father, also Mr Jim Norton, in 1932. The Nortons delivered coal to Exton, Clyst St Mary, outlying farmers and Topsham people.

THE KETCH *JULIE* ON THE RIVER DART in the 1930s. The *Julie* carried an engine and was owned by Mr Bannin Voysey of Topsham. Built of teak at Malpas, and of 70 tons, the *Julie* was a general trader. She was sold to a retired naval officer from Guernsey and lost shortly afterwards off Eddystone. Members of the Voysey family owned many other similar vessels in the early part of this century, such as the *Confidence* of Rye bought by W. Voysey in 1900, a ketch of 73 tons.

MR WILLIAM VOYSEY AND MR GEORGE VOYSEY with their seine-net. These two brothers are said to be the two last full-time fishermen working from Topsham. The two men are standing in front of the Fishermen's Causeway (or 'Causey'), which was built by Captain Tom Holman in 1922 with help from the Market House Trust. (Photographs courtesy of Mr E. Voysey.)

LIMEKILNS OPPOSITE THE DOCK, in use, together with kilns to the south of the Quay, from the early seventeenth century. The limestone was carried by boat from the huge shelf of Long Rock at Babbacombe and from Berry Head, Brixham. The culm came from South Wales. Lime was used for whitewashing houses, both inside and out, and also extensively as an agricultural fertilizer.

THE KETCH *MISTLETOE*. Built at Plymouth in 1890, the *Mistletoe* was a regular visitor to Topsham, seen here bringing limestone to the Dock in the 1930s with Mr Bill Trout on deck. The Dock was then owned by Heywoods, who succeeded G. Hurdle & Sons (founded in 1820), who were 'Lime, Coal, Salt and Manure Merchants'. A steam crane was used to unload the cargo, which was then carried by a horse pulling a two-wheeled cart to the top of the kiln. The limestone was put in the kiln in alternate layers with the culm or coal and then the kiln was fired to produce the lime.

THE *ANNIE*, a smack belonging to Mr James Voysey, sen., in the Cut to the north of the Quay in 1947. Mr Reg Chambers is at the winch and Mr Roy Turner is by the bucket. The mud which was dredged to keep the channel clear was used to strengthen the banks of the canal.

THE LAUNCH OF *MFV 268*. Stansbury of Plymouth set up this yard temporarily at the Recreation Ground, Topsham, during the war years and built six of these motor fishing vessels using some women workers.

A BRIGANTINE, square-rigged on the foremast, is drawn by horse along the Exeter Canal. The photograph is from a glass negative. Exeter Canal was extended to Turf in 1827, making a total length of the canal of 5¼ miles. The work was carried out by engineer James Green, Surveyor of Bridges and Buildings for the County of Devon, who, at the same time, built a new lock at Topsham to replace the one at Lower Sluice, and a lock-keeper's cottage, which was completed in 1832.

In the early fourteenth century the Countess of Devon had built weirs to improve her fisheries at 'Wear' on the Exe, but it was her successor, Hugh Courtenay, who blocked the river passage completely, thus denying vessels access to the city of Exeter from the sea. The original Exeter Canal was built in 1564–6 and was some two miles in length, allowing vessels to avoid the obstruction at 'Countess Wear' and to re-establish Exeter's link with the sea. James Green's extension of the canal to Turf was the last stage in a series of improvements to the original canal.

LOCK COTTAGE, C. 1900. In some isolation, between the canal and the river, Lock Cottage was lived in continuously until c. 1946. Mr Robert Howard (below) was the lock-keeper for many years. His daughter, Mrs Mary Warner, followed him in taking vessels through Topsham Lock. For many years Bill and Bob Irish, nephews of Mrs Warner, lived at Lock Cottage. As children they had to row across the river to go to school in Topsham, as did Valerie Tupper and her two brothers from Turf, who had a much longer journey to school by water.

VIEW OF TOPSHAM from the west bank of the canal. The yacht moored by the canal bank belonged to Mr Charles Ross, one-time Mayor of Exeter.

TURF HOUSE AND LOCK. The entrance to Exeter Canal from the sea is at Turf. From 1910 to 1918 the lock-keeper at Turf was Captain W.C. Davey, who, in his younger days, had voyaged all over the world in square-riggers. As well as working the lock, the Daveys served cream teas or 'whitebait' teas, sometimes for as many as three hundred people in one afternoon.

REPAIRING THE LOCK GATES AT TURF. The photograph is of the late Mr Reg Trout, a shipwright, who was in charge of repair work to the canal.

THE *LEADER*, built at Mr Evans' shipyard at Salcombe in 1869, is shown here as a brigantine. After many years trading, the *Leader* was bought by Mr William Trout. In 1918, while Mr Trout was working with his father Mr Daniel Trout, a tragic accident occurred which brought about the death of Mr Daniel Trout. The *Leader* was then towed across the river, pushed into the bank and left there.

DECAYING VESSELS line the banks of the canal. Between the wars it became increasingly expensive to carry on coastal trade and many vessels were abandoned. These three old hulks were photographed in 1934 by Mr Grahame Farr.

TWO VIEWS FROM THE CANAL BANK FEATURING THE HULKS. The photograph, *The Waterfront at Topsham*, is shown by kind permission of the Bodleian Library, Oxford. (J.J. Postcards, Devon, No. 42752. By courtesy of Ms J.A. Wilson.) The view below is by kind permission of the West Country Studies Library, Exeter.

MENDING NETS AT THE GALLOWS. A traditional scene (above) of fishermen mending their nets by the 'gallows' at the foot of the churchyard wall. Before the First World War there were some thirty fishing boats working on the river. The fishermen used to bark and tar the old nets after use. Mr Robert Bolt (1880–1969) is seen mending his seine-net (below), c. 1935.

FISHERMAN AND FOOTBALLER, MR DICK 'PINCHER' PYM is here shown repairing his fishing net. Mr Pym was born in Ferry Road, Topsham, in 1893. He started fishing when he was fifteen years old, but his talent for football soon brought him into the public eye. He played for Exeter City before joining Bolton Wanderers. He went on to play in three Cup Finals at Wembley, in 1923, 1926 and 1929, at which he did not concede a single goal. Returning to Topsham in 1934, Mr Pym took up fishing again.

MR AND MRS PYM. This photograph in Topsham Museum shows Mr Pym wearing a guernsey made in Topsham. The style is rather plain, like that worn by most fishermen here. Some of the women used to knit such sweaters on umbrella spokes.

SALMON FISHING. The series of photographs on this and the opposite page depicts a timeless scene of fishermen trimming the seine-net and hauling in the catch (see p. 54).

THE HARVEST. Mr Joe Newman, Mr 'Lovey' Pym, Mr 'Goaty' Edworthy, Mr Jim Bowers and Mr Bill Newman with their catch. The working day for fishermen starts when the tide begins to ebb. The net is cast as the river bank begins to show. Extremely long seine-nets are used, which are about seven feet in depth at each end, increasing to about twenty feet in the middle. A salmon boat carries the net across the river away from the shoreman making a great semi-circle. The series of photographs on the previous page (taken in the early 1950s) shows the fishermen trimming the net and slowly hauling in the catch. A salmon-fishing licence is held by one man in a team of five fishermen, and the profits are traditionally divided between them with one extra share to defray the expense of the boat.

THE LARGEST SALMON CAUGHT ON THE EXE. This enormous salmon, weighing 61¼lb, was caught in 1924 by Mr Richard Voysey, Mr Jim Voysey and his nephew, also called Jim Voysey. The fish is preserved in the R.A.M. Museum, Exeter.

SALMON SUPPER. Mr and Mrs Roy Wheeler are here enjoying a salmon supper, an annual event, organized for many years by the Trefoil Guild of Topsham.

SIR ALEXANDER HAMILTON, the last 'squire' of Topsham, who died in 1929. Topsham people remember his kindness. The Girl Guides were allowed to camp in the ballroom at the Retreat for example. A popular riverside path, Sir Alex Walk, preserves his name.

THE RETREAT, viewed here across the reed beds, lies half a mile to the north of Topsham and is accessible from the river. The first buildings on this site included a sugar refinery and distillery built by Mr Samuel Buttall. He was a sugar baker with estates in South Carolina who came to live in Topsham from Plymouth in the late seventeenth century.

Topsham men have always claimed a traditional right to cut spires (reeds) for thatching. This right was challenged in 1863 by Mr S.J. Kekewich, MP, who lived in Exminster. Messrs Edward Jenkins, John Bass, and John Ellis, all of Topsham, were summoned for having trespassed on Mr Kekewich's land, and for having appropriated spires. The defence argued that it had been the custom of Topsham people for upwards of fifty years to cut spires for their own use, commenting that, 'At times the water in the river rose five feet high on the spire beds, and indeed vessels sailed over them'. Mr Kekewich must have lost his case, as Mr Morice Parsons remembers in the 1920s seeing boats coming down the river full of spires with only about four inches of freeboard above the water.

SECTION TWO
The Town

TOPSHAM FROM THE AIR, C. 1939. A general view southwards across the town. The main street – first High Street, then Fore Street – threads its way down to the Quay. In the foreground, on both sides of the street, are market gardens. The river channel, seen at low tide, passes close to the shore. On the far side of the river some derelict vessels lie abandoned in the mud.

ENTRANCE TO PYNES' HIGH STREET GARDENS, the home of Mr and Mrs Ted Pyne. This building was demolished c. 1979 to make way for a new housing development. Another member of the family, Mr George Pyne, owned the Denver Nurseries. In the early 1900s the Pynes were major employers in Topsham. They specialized in growing soft fruit, such as gooseberries, raspberries and also asparagus. Their produce was sent by train to Covent Garden. Archaeological discoveries have been made on land belonging to the Pynes, which have indicated a Roman settlement in the area to the north of the town. Below: Pynes' lorry is driven by Mr George Mortimore, with Mr Harry Gould on the right.

TURNERS EXETER INN, still thatched today. A street scene in the early 1900s looking north towards the Exeter Road. The horse and cart stands just by the entrance to Denver Road, formerly Pound Lane. (Photograph courtesy of Devon Library Services)

PRINGS EXETER INN. The unusually shaped tree ahead was a landmark for more than a hundred years. The tall metal posts on the left, in two sections, were to carry electricity wires. Later the transmission was put underground.

A PERFORMING BEAR in Topsham High Street, c. 1907. (From Miss Cecily Goodman's photograph album.)

THE APPROACH TO TOPSHAM, looking south along the High Street in the 1940s. The entrance to Pynes' Nursery Gardens is on the left. Beyond is the Topsham Building Company with a circular advertisement, and next door with the awning is Mr Tickle's butcher's shop. The car is parked outside Denley's dairy, formerly a dairy owned by Mr Alfred Bridle.

THE OLD SMITHY, ASHFORD ROAD. Mr Ted Hutchings in his forge, surrounded by the tools of his trade which he had made himself. Mr Hutchings was also a carpenter and wheelwright. He moved to Topsham in 1919, first renting the buildings for £20 a year before buying them. At one time he had some 250 horses to shoe: farm horses, delivery ponies, the horses from Topsham Barracks, hacks and hunters as well as the old grey mare which delivered for the railway. It was the 'age of the horse'. After Mr Hutchings died, his premises, shown below, were sold and the land redeveloped.

MITCHELL'S TEA ROOMS, HIGH STREET. Mr George Mitchell, in his white coat, is talking to the driver of the car. The High Street here leads north into the main Exeter Road. On the left is the Lord Nelson Inn, pictured below. Note the pump to the right of the building.

STREET SCENE AT THE NORTH END OF FORE STREET, c. 1900. The lad wears a yoke to support the two buckets of milk he is delivering. On the right stands Grove House, home of Mr John Holman, the nineteenth-century shipbuilder. The same scene below shows a policeman standing on the left and a pony and trap entering the town. The lamplighter, possibly Mr Harry Towell, lit and snuffed the eighty-five public gas mantles each day. The Topsham Gas and Coke Company was established in 1849 in White Street and the works chimney was a landmark in Topsham for many years.

THE MATTHEWS HALL was opened in 1927 by Mr Woodrow Matthews. The ceremony to lay the foundation stone, pictured below, shows Mr Matthews standing on the left accompanied by Dr Ashford. Mr Matthews had worked for the Holman family for many years and, on returning to Topsham, bought Grove House. His concern was to build this public hall for the people of Topsham. The site had previously been occupied by a farm owned by Mr 'Fiddle' Hurdle. The Hurdle's farmhouse still stands on the opposite side of Fore Street.

VIEW OF FORE STREET, FACING NORTH. The model of the Penny Farthing is above Shorlands shop. Horse and cart transport left the roads in an undesirable state!

A SEVENTEENTH-CENTURY HOUSE, now the Bon-Bon shop, housed the Moggeridge family, who were shipmasters trading with Holland. Still to be seen in the porch are attractive Delft tiles dating from those days. A court, first known as Moggeridge's, later Swain's Court, lies behind this building. Such courts are typical of Topsham, each having a communal pump.

MRS RICHARDS outside the family's baker's shop (above left). The old ovens (left) were removed from the shop in the 1960s. C.J. Gale owned the shop some years before this, which shows this was an old-established bakery business. (Photographs by kind permission of Mrs Gwen Stoneman).

UNDERHILLS (above right). This shop has changed hands twice since belonging to Underhills. The lane which runs back along the south side of the shop is still known as 'Underhills Court'.

WHITE'S, FAMILY BUTCHERS, established 1838. The cards advertise 'Devon Heifers' from Crediton, 'Prime Devon Ox' from Nether Exe and 'Prime Exmoor Beef' from a Clyst St George farmer.

HOPEWELLS. The seven round-headed windows on the right were once a feature of Topsham's market. Early this century Hopewells were tenants of the Market House Trust, a charity whose income derived from this property and from investments. After maintaining the building itself, the trustees used, and still use, their income to help worthwhile causes in Topsham. In 1867 the two-storey part of the building became the local police station, with a residence for a police constable and a lock-up house with cells for prisoners.

THE LONDON AND SOUTH WESTERN HOTEL was built by George Gale, an excise officer from Hampshire, who settled in Topsham in the early 1800s. Mr Charles Gale, his son, married Miss Tryphena Sparkes of Plymouth in 1877. Earlier Tryphena had been engaged to the writer Thomas Hardy, who, in his poetry, often refers to 'his lost love'. After her early death at the age of thirty-nine, Topsham was visited by Hardy and his brother when they came to see Tryphena's grave.

OLD COTTAGES IN MAJORFIELD ROAD, off Fore Street.

TOPSHAM POST OFFICE at No. 76 Fore Street, between c. 1878 and 1905. *White's Directory* of 1878 describes its functions as 'Post, Money Order, Telegraph Office, Savings Bank and Government Annuity Insurance Office at Mr. Robert H. Pollard's'. The young lady on the right of the photograph is Miss Annie Drew, later Mrs Bray. The building is now occupied by Lloyds Bank.

POST OFFICE ON THE CORNER OF MAJORFIELD ROAD. A man is standing with his hand in his pocket outside the post office as it was in around 1905. A secret cupboard was discovered when the cottages were altered, which contained a pair of seventeenth-century shoes, now on display at Topsham Museum.

THE SALUTATION HOTEL. A pony and trap are here seen emerging from the Salutation Hotel yard into Fore Street, this part of which lacks pavements. An old coaching inn, with a cobbled courtyard, pump and stables, which has recently been redeveloped, the Salutation has a bowling-green at the back which overlooks the river and which dates back to at least the seventeenth century. The projecting wing at the front, containing a room now used for billiards, was formerly an Assembly Room. The Venetian window with broken pediment facing the road is an attractive feature. The photograph below shows the Helmore's Salutation Hotel at a later date. Here the street is paved, with tall metal poles shown on the left, carrying the electricity supply on overhead wires.

TOPSHAM INFANTS, MAJORFIELD ROAD. Delightful expressions are shown on the faces of the children from Class III. The girls are wearing traditional white pinafores, and many of the boys lace collars. For many years both the infants' school and the school for girls shared these premises. The north wing of the building was a Quaker meeting house from around 1714. It was used as a Wesleyan chapel from 1811, and as a school by 1852.

TOPSHAM GIRLS' SCHOOL in 1898, photographed outside the entrance gate to the school.

ST NICHOLAS' METHODIST CHURCH, built in 1867 by the architect J.R.N. Haswell of North Shields in a rather unusual style. Among its supporters were Mr John Holman, the shipbuilder, and his family. Stained-glass memorial windows inside record the loss at sea of some Topsham-built vessels and their crews.

COMMUNION PLATE FROM THE OLD PRESBYTERIAN CHAPEL. The plate shown on the left is now at the Meadville Theological School in Chicago. In the eighteenth century it belonged to the Presbyterian chapel in Victoria Road. In the early 1700s some 600 supporters worshipped there, among them many shipmasters who had prospered through Topsham's trade with Holland.

CONGREGATIONAL CHAPELS. The first Independent chapel (below left) in Topsham was a meeting place for Congregationalists from 1804. A new Congregational chapel (below right) was built in Victoria Road in 1839. The Scottish missionary to Africa, Miss Mary Slessor, who visited her mother and sister, who were living in Topsham, in 1885 and 1891, attended this chapel while she was here. On both occasions, she brought with her Janie, her adopted African daughter.

HARVEST FESTIVALS at the Congregational chapel. In the picture above, dated 1924, the organist, Miss Mary Greenslade, may be seen next to the minister, Mr Challis. Below them, from the left, are Mr Reg Pym, Mr Radford, Mr Seward and Mr George Harris. A beautiful harvest festival display in the chapel is shown in the picture below.

THE PARISH CHURCH, 1874, AND AFTER 1878. Above may be seen the church as it was after it had been rebuilt in 1676. Only the tower remained of the earlier fifteenth-century church. Below, the church is seen as it is today and as it was rebuilt by the architect Mr Edward Ashford between 1876 and 1878. The photograph shows that railings then separated the church from the burial ground.

ST MARGARET'S CHURCH FROM THE RIVER. The parish church is built on the top of sandstone cliffs which are protected by a strong retaining wall. The view from the cliff top over the river to the Haldon Hills is of great natural beauty. The first known church on the site was built by the Normans, but only the font now remains of this building. St Margaret of Antioch, the patron saint, was martyred c. AD 275. Her crime was to refuse to give up her Christian faith in order to marry the Roman governor of the province. The Topsham parish registers, 1600–1837, in two bound volumes with an index, (Devon and Cornwall Record Society, 1938) are available in the Topsham Museum.

THE OLD VICARAGE. Situated in what is now Monmouth Avenue, this attractive Regency house was first used as a vicarage in the early 1860s. The Revd John Arundell Leakey (1857–88) was the first clergyman to live here. The building was demolished in 1917.

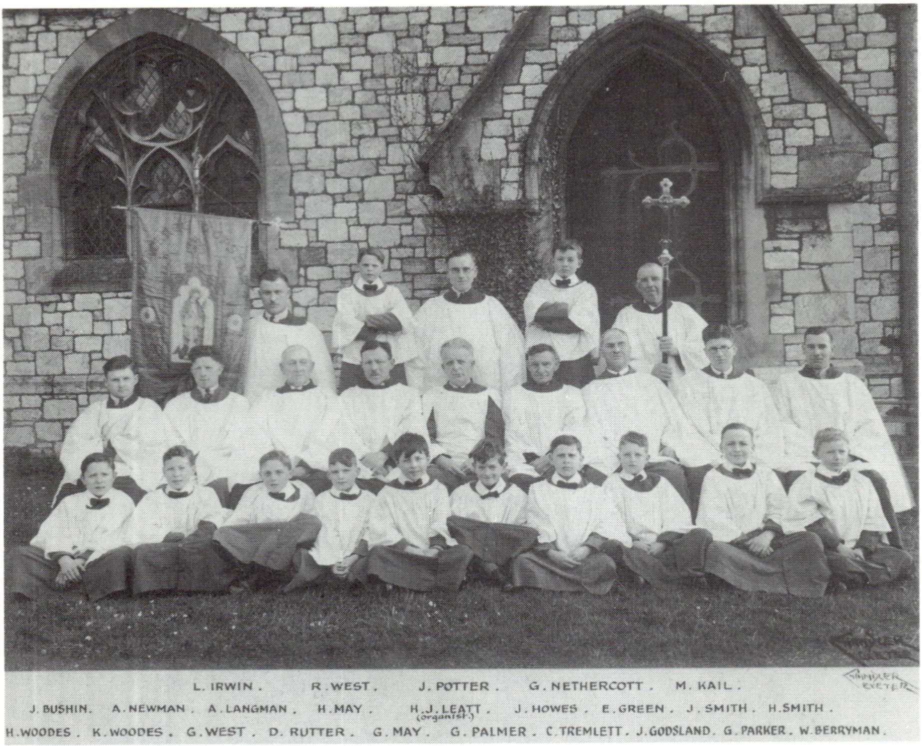
L. IRWIN. R. WEST. J. POTTER. G. NETHERCOTT. M. KAIL.
J. BUSHIN. A. NEWMAN. A. LANGMAN. H. MAY. H. J. LEATT (organist). J. HOWES. E. GREEN. J. SMITH. H. SMITH.
H. WOODES. K. WOODES. G. WEST. D. RUTTER. G. MAY. G. PALMER. C. TREMLETT. J. GODSLAND. G. PARKER. W. BERRYMAN.

ST MARGARET'S CHURCH CHOIR, 1936. Mr Lionel Irwin, the choirmaster for many years, is carrying the banner.

FRY'S
PURE COCOA
FRY'S
CHOCOLATE

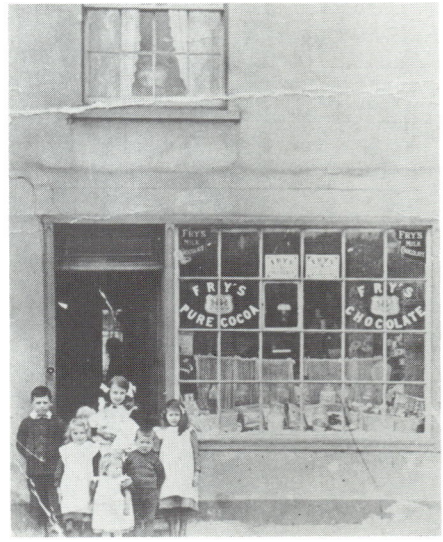

THE IRWIN FAMILY. Mr Lionel Irwin is shown here as a baby with his brothers and sisters.

BAKERIES IN THE 1930s. Before the Second World War there were five baker's shops in Topsham: W.F. Tucker & Son (on the left), R.E. Pym (below), Courtiers, R.F. Richards and Parsons. Bread deliveries used to be made daily but this was stopped during the war. W.F. Tucker and R.F. Richards had both town and country deliveries. Mr Morice Parsons has described how flour and a whole range of goods used to come in far greater bulk than today. Flour came in sacks or half-sacks. A whole sack of flour weighed 280 lb. Sugar came in 2 cwt bags. Before the war it was a customary service for bakers to cook dinners for families, especially in the summer when fires would not have been lit.

ONE OF A ROW OF SEVENTEENTH-CENTURY HOUSES in Fore Street, viewed from Trees Court, showing original architectural features, including a decorated rainwaterhead.

ST MARGARET'S TERRACE, an interesting area near the church. Through the entrance is seen a cobbled yard. To the right is perhaps the oldest building in the town, with its medieval, sandstone door arch just visible. On the left through the entrance but out of sight stand the Church Rooms, where a soup kitchen was set up in 1889, recorded by the *Exeter & Plymouth Gazette:* 'Topsham. The soup kitchen is to be open tomorrow. It is much needed owing to the extreme dullness of the season'. Times could be hard in Topsham.

RADFORD'S GLOBE HOTEL C. 1900. In 1866 the Globe Hotel was described as a 'commercial and family hotel, posting house and Inland Revenue office', and an 'importer of Cornish and Welsh slate'. An old coaching inn with stables at the back, the Globe has had an interesting history.

IN FESTIVE MOOD. Mr Fred R. Nott, grandfather of the present proprietor, Mr W.A. Nott, is standing in the doorway in his long, white apron. Mr Nott first came to Topsham as an apprentice and returned in 1914 to buy the business. The building itself is of interest: constructed in 1708 by Mr John Burridge, a shipmaster engaged in trade to Holland, it was then called 'The Green House'. Later the premises were used as the custom-house until 1862. The customs boats were kept on davits on the river side of the building below the former Woolcombes' sail loft.

L. WARE'S BAKERY in 1907, with Miss Gertrude Ware standing in the doorway. Miss Ware was soon to marry Mr Frederick Morrish Parsons of Tedburn St Mary. On the right is shown the shop-window at a later date. Mr Morice Parsons was born here and followed his parents into the bakery business until he retired in 1960. Mr Parsons has served as an Independent councillor for Topsham on Exeter City Council since July 1977.

MISS GERTRUDE PARSONS, dressed for work in the bakery during the First World War while her husband was away in the forces. The house and bakery later took the name 'Ship Aground' because a ship had, long ago, been driven ashore and lodged itself against this building.

SAIL LOFT, WHITE STREET. This first-floor timbered building was an old sail loft. A family lived in the house beneath.

DUTCH COURT, off Monmouth Hill. Small, two-inch Dutch bricks may be seen in small quantities in chimney stacks and walls all round Topsham. Here the whole south façade of the building is made from these small bricks or 'clinkers'. Such bricks were brought as ballast in the seventeenth century when vessels were returning empty from Holland after shipping out serge cloth, but were also brought over as normal cargo and sold for building purposes.

THE STRAND, 1906: the most celebrated street in Topsham, with its series of 'handsome houses' built between 1680 and 1730, unique in the south-west because of their characteristic Dutch-style gables. Small riverside gardens lie behind the railings (to the left). The Strand houses show the prosperity which came to Topsham through the export of Devonshire-made serge cloth in the seventeenth and eighteenth centuries.

TWO VIEWS ALONG THE STRAND, looking south. The old Dutch House (right) is covered in Virginia creeper while, beyond, The Elms is shown as it was in the early 1900s, before the first floor was removed. The picture on the left shows a more typical Dutch-style house.

THE HOLMAN CHILDREN in front of The Elms in 1869. Tom Holman is in the push-chair. The four adults are looking after the children. The photograph is from an original daguerreotype, enhanced by the attractive frame.

IN FRONT OF THE ELMS is the car which belonged to Mr 'Chuggy' Amos, who lived here in the early 1900s. It is thought to be a De Dion Bouton.

EIGHTEENTH CENTURY CHERUBS. These ornamental drainpipes can be seen at No. 3 Higher Shapter Street, and in the museum garden at No. 25 The Strand.

LOOKING BACK ALONG THE STRAND from the Goat Walk, 'Sea View', home of the late Captain Tom Holman, is seen on the left. The railings have since been removed, probably during the war.

'SEA VIEW', the home of Captain Tom Holman from the air. These two photographs come from a scrapbook compiled by Mr William Harrison, who met Capt. Holman on board the *Duchess of York*, bound for Canada in 1937. Capt. Holman describes his home: 'My grandfather and father were building ships where my home now stands. I filled up the slips and made a garden round the house in 1902.' (Capt. Holman's grandfather was Mr John Holman and his father Mr Richard Holman.)

MACKEREL FISHING in the 1930s. Captain Tom Holman on one of his boats. 'Captain Tom' was well-liked – a born raconteur. He was fourteen years old when he made his first voyage to America and he spent the early part of his life at sea visiting all parts of the globe. He used to say he had never earned one pound on land in his life. (These two photographs by kind permission of Mrs G. Gullidge.)

STRAND HOUSES FROM THE RIVER. Most Strand houses have riverside gardens, with open places where boats were beached. This photograph shows one of the small summer-houses of the kind fashionable in the nineteenth century. Through the trees, one can distinguish The Elms and Reka Dom.

THE GOATWALK FROM RIVERSMEET. The idea of building a 'beach path' from the end of the Strand, south to Riversmeet, was put forward in 1908 to the Market House Trust. Funds were made available for the purpose and the path was completed in 1912. The path has been known as the Goatwalk from that time.

INCISED STONES AT RIVERSMEET. In 1950 Mr L.E. Braddick photographed these stones found on the north shore of the River Clyst, immediately outside the high wall which encloses Riversmeet. Most of the stones have 'F. Davy' marked on them, referring to Mr Francis Davy (1810–96), the youngest son of Mr Robert Davy, shipbuilder, of Countess Wear, an 'Iron and Hemp Merchant'. Mr Davy built a retaining wall round the marshlands to the south of Topsham in the 1840s and for himself he built Riversmeet House. The stone above reads:

AT THIS SPOT WAS BUILT BY MR SAUNDERS, A.D. 1782, THE DEVONSHIRE MERCHANT VESSEL, 200 TONS BURTHEN ALSO THE FAWN FRIGATE 22 GUNS AND 300 TONS BURTHEN FOR H.M. NAVY, A.D. 1806 ALSO A VESSEL OF ABOUT 80 TONS A NEWFOUNDLAND BANKER. THE TWO LAST NAMED VESSELS WERE CONSTRUCTED BY MR THO. OWENS, JNR.

ELM GROVE ROAD AND NEWCOURT ROAD. The approach to Topsham from the east is along the Clyst Road – where one could find original milestones – then into Elm Grove Road. The photograph of Elm Grove Road (above, left) reflects a peaceful scene at the turn of the century. The photograph above right shows Mrs Mortimore outside her Newcourt Road cottage, c. 1900, with her daughter on a rocking horse. Her friend with the bicycle is Miss Ella Knight. This building has since been demolished.

THE CATHOLIC CHURCH OF THE HOLY CROSS, on Station Road, just off Elm Grove Road. The church was built in 1936 to the specification of the Very Reverend Canon Cahill, who was priest here until 1953.

BUILDING THE SHRUBBERY for Captain Harry Holman in the 1880s. The workmen on the scaffolding are wearing bowler hats – perhaps the safety helmets of the period?

ALTAMIRA, a spacious Victorian dwelling built in the 1880s on the eastern outskirts of the town, was surrounded by a beautiful garden and had a field beyond. Altamira Lodge on Monmouth Street still stands, although the house itself was demolished in 1963 to make way for the present housing estate. Miss Addy Hellier remembers playing at Altamira as a child, when Mrs Wimbush owned the property. She later joined the 'Busy Bees' who met in the evenings at the church room but afterwards in the dining room at Altamira. The young people worked for Peshawar, India, making Red Cross caps, aprons, bandages and 'pneumonia jackets', which were specially padded.

THE BRIDGE INN. The road leads on over the bridge to Exmouth, through Exton and Lympstone. An early painting of the Bridge Inn shows a plain rectangular structure; the projecting wing to the south was added later. In front of the inn (below) is Mr D.K. Norton's coal cart. The River Clyst at nearly high tide curves round to Odam's manure and chemical factory (see p. 39). The factory's chimney (demolished in 1940) can be seen in the background.

THE CLYST BRIDGE was built by Mr Andrew Parker around 1745.

VIEW OF BRIDGE MILLS ACROSS THE RIVER CLYST. This working mill, which used water power until 1960, today mixes animal foods. The weir across the river, which gathered and channelled the waters into the mill-pond behind the mill, may be seen. From the road one can see the wheel pit where the large water wheel once stood, driven by a leat from the waters collected in the pond.

INTERIOR OF BRIDGE MILLS AND THE OLD SUN FIRE MARK. The mill dates back to at least 1787, the year when an insurance policy was taken out by Mr James Woodman of Clyst St George for £700. The annual premium was 17s.

G. & E.J. FISHER'S LORRY, C. 1924. The lorry stands in front of the mill. The driver is Mr Bill Rowe.

SECTION THREE

The Surrounding Area: Countess Wear, Clyst St George, Ebford and Exton, Lympstone

COUNTESS WEAR BRIDGE. Until 1774, when a bridge was built for the first time at Countess Wear, the lowest bridging point across the River Exe was two miles to the north, in Exeter. The new bridge of seven arches was built by Mr Thomas Parker of Topsham. Two of the arches were converted into one in 1842 by Mr Robert Davy at a cost of £430, 'for better passage for his barges particularly during floods'.

Mr Francis Davy, in a biography of his father Robert Davy, wrote of the time before the bridge was built 'when three men and a horse were drowned in one day in endeavouring to ford the river when floods and tide were high, they being strangers'.

THE POPLARS, the home of Mr Robert Davy (1762–1862), was built around 1789. Described by his son Francis as 'the largest limeburner, coal merchant and shipbuilder in the West of England' between the years 1790 and 1825 Robert Davy was an entrepreneur who brought employment to the area. From repairing stone barges which supplied materials for his lime kilns, he went on to build a variety of sailing vessels, including some for the East India Company, first at Glasshouse, later at Gulpit, in Countess Wear. During the Napoleonic Wars Mr Davy built warships for the navy. The house still stands, but is much altered. It now belongs to the British Rheumatism and Arthritis Association.

COUNTESS WEAR VILLAGE. This picturesque cluster of thatched cottages near the River Exe is the nucleus of the old 'hamlet of Wear'. Many industries flourished here, using the resources of the river. Stone boats of the Davys used to unload at the quay in front of the limekilns (to the left of the photograph). Paper mills situated upstream from these kilns, in operation from 1704, continued to provide work until 1885.

THATCHED HOUSE, GLASSHOUSE LANE, the site of the old glass works. This photograph by Mr R. Hares shows the attractive seventeenth-century house from the direction of the river. Glass was made here by Mr William Reynell of Topsham, who died in 1702. His wife, Elizabeth, advertised in the *London Gazette* the same year: 'To let – A Round Bottle Glass House 94 foot high and 60 foot broad.' The glass house was demolished in the eighteenth century.

ST LUKE'S CHAPEL, COUNTESS WEAR, was consecrated in November 1838. Until this time the nearest church to the village of Countess Wear was in Topsham. In 1844 the chapel became a parish church, but Countess Wear continued as part of the civil parish of Topsham until 1894 when both places became part of the new St Thomas Rural District Council.

COUNTESS WEAR HOUSE AND GROUNDS from the west bank of the River Exe.

NEWCOURT HOUSE. A charming pastoral scene with sheep grazing in front of the house. Donne's map of 1765 shows Newcourt with 'Shapley Esqre' as the owner. Today Newcourt is used as a hospital.

FARMING AT SANDYGATE. These two photographs of the appropriately named Hayman Farm, situated near Clyst St Mary, were taken in 1908. The first, of tea-time in the hayfield, depicts 'Grandfather Hayman' holding the horse and grandmother with the tea-basket. Grandfather (with beard) is also featured in the next stage of the operation – building the haystack.

THE ROUND HOUSE, SANDYGATE, a former toll-house, which was demolished to make way for the widening of the Exeter – Sidmouth Road in around 1937. Another former toll-house, Newport Lodge, once known as 'Loggerheads', still stands on the Exeter – Exmouth Road, half a mile to the north of Topsham. Toll-houses used also to stand next to the bridge at Countess Wear and by the George and Dragon at Clyst St George.

THE PARISH CHURCH OF CLYST ST MARY. This picture of the parish church is dated 1799 and shows the present tower and small nave. The church stands some distance from the village of Clyst St Mary with its ancient bridge. The position of the church suggests it was a private chapel of the lord of the manor.

THE PARISH CHURCH OF CLYST ST GEORGE. The manor of Clyst St George (then called Clisewic) is mentioned in the Domesday Book. The chancel of the stone church was built about 1300 and the tower and nave about 1420, but the list of rectors goes back as far as 1238 without interruption. The Revd H.T. Ellacombe (1790–1885) was a particularly notable incumbent. He became rector of Clyst St George in 1850, having formerly worked as an engineer for Marc Brunel, the father of Isambard Kingdom Brunel. He immediately set about refurbishing the church, which he found 'to be in a bad state of repair'. His restoration of the tower included the installation of a peal of six bells. A campanologist himself, he invented a system which could be rung single-handed. This he did after he had banned the regular ringers from the belfry for being drunk on duty.

INTERIOR, LOOKING TOWARDS THE TOWER. The church is still using candlelight, and probably looks much as it did after Revd Ellacombe had completed his refurbishments.

THE CHURCH WITH THE NEW OIL LAMPS INSTALLED. Although a little later, this record of the elaborately decorated interior may be noted and contrasted with the photograph on p. 154, showing the effects of enemy action in 1940.

THE OLD STOCKS still to be found in the churchyard at Clyst St George.

PUPILS OF LADY SEWARD SCHOOL, CLYST ST GEORGE in 1924. The school was founded by Lady Seward in 1704/5 in accordance with the will of her late husband Sir Edward Seward of Clyst Court. The purpose was 'to instruct the children of Clyst St George in the principles of holy Christian faith and religion and to teach them writing, arithmetic and navigation'. The importance of a knowledge of navigation reflects the link between these outlying villages and Topsham, then a flourishing trading and fishing port.

FIRST WORLD WAR GIFT CERTIFICATE. These were awarded to pupils of the school who collected money for the troops.

SCHOOL OUTING AT PYTTE HOUSE, 1908. In happier times the Gibbs family, who were great benefactors to the village, allowed the school to use the grounds of their home for the annual outing. Miss Betty Gibbs, now aged eighty-five, remembers the fun and games at these events, including the buns being distributed, and the races in which she and her brothers and sister loved to take part.

PYTTE HOUSE, C. 1908. Owned by the Gibbs family since 1560, and occupied by Antony Hubert and Mary Mercy Gibbs from 1899, the house was extended and an upper storey added in 1912. The family, at one time involved in the export of wool to Spain, and later in the import of guano for use a fertilizer, also founded the firm of Antony Gibbs & Sons in the City of London.

PYTTE HOUSE in 1912.

EVAN GIBBS in 1906/7, photographed by his father, who was a keen early photographer, and whose efforts have given us this unique record of Edwardian family life.

BETTY GIBBS in 1906.

Right:
ELAINE WITH HER MOTHER, MARY MERCY GIBBS, on the tennis-court at Pytte House in 1903.

BETTY GIBBS IN HER PRAM. In fact this was an early version of a push-chair, and the lower end folded down to allow an older child to sit more comfortably.

THE SAND PIT. The yards of starched lace and petticoats did not prevent Betty and her sister Elaine and cousin Alexander enjoying themselves in the sand pit in the care of 'Nana' Trowbridge. A cart transported sand each year from Exmouth beach to furnish this pit which was situated under the oak tree in the grounds of their home.

THE CRICKET PICNIC, 1911. Pytte House was also the venue for the Cricket Week, which took place each summer until the First World War.

SHOOTING PARTY AT CLYST ST GEORGE. This picture was gleaned from the album of the late Mr William John Gibbings, whose family own and run the Bridge Inn, and who was clerk at Clyst St George Church for fifty years.

THE HUNT in 1948, climbing the hill to Clyst St George. In the background on the right can be seen the George & Dragon, where they met twice a year until 1973. On warm days they were fortified with a glass of sherry, and if the weather was inclement Mr Bill Moor, the publican, offered a glass of brandy.

MODEL COTTAGES AT CLYST ST GEORGE, c. 1900. Mrs Antony Gibbs can be seen in the foreground, and it was her husband who had rebuilt the cottages in 1863, much against the wishes of one of the tenants who preferred the original thatched property. Two cottages were allocated to each of the farms on Mr Gibb's estate to accommodate employees. More recently a post office was run in the end cottage by Mrs Tucker, and her family were responsible for the topiary work that can just be detected in the front garden.

EBFORD MANOR in the late 1930s. The exterior of this grade II listed building has changed little since it was built in 1710 for Mr Robert Venn, a wealthy wool merchant from a Topsham family. The style is classical like that of the new customs house in Exeter built a few years earlier, but the bricks were made locally – possibly at a site 200 yd down the road called 'brick field' in 1839. The connection with the local woollen cloth trade continued when Mr Matthew Lee, a nephew of Mr Robert Venn, inherited the property in 1728. Mr Lee, a very influential merchant trading with Holland, was also treasurer of the Exeter Whale Fishery Company. He was one of the two principal backers of Benjamin Donne's pioneering venture to produce a map of the county of Devon in 1765. His name, home, and the pleasure house that he built on the hill to the south of the manor to watch his ships returning to port in Topsham, are all clearly marked on the map. He was a supporter of the Gulliford Meeting at Lympstone, and is likely to have been involved in the building of Gulliford chapel in 1774 (see p. 116), the style and materials of which are similar to those of the manor.

THE COLLACOTT FAMILY in 1905, photographed in the vegetable garden outside their home, Rose Cott, in the top lane at Ebford. Mr Joseph Collacott was the local carpenter, wheelwright and undertaker and worked in an outbuilding behind the cottage.

FARMER TROUT WITH HIS WIFE AND SIX DAUGHTERS in front of the sixteenth-century Ebford Barton farmhouse, where he farmed in the early years of this century. The farmhouse, originally built by the Haydon family of Woodbury, was later farmed by tenants when the Haydons became related to the Venn and Lee families through marriage and went on to occupy Ebford Manor which adjoins the old farmhouse.

ALFORD'S FARM, EXTON, 1894/5. For many centuries farming was the main occupation in the hinterland of Topsham, both to provide for the local population and to supply the ships. This farm, run for many generations by the Alford family, is situated on the main A376 Exeter to Exmouth road, but the photograph was taken in the days when the road was little more than a track. The small child seated on the wall in front of the Elizabethan farmhouse is Mr William Alford.

HORSE-DRAWN BINDER, C. 1934, driven by Mr William Alford, and pulled by Prince, Violet and Damsel. It is working in School Field (opposite the old Exton school) and is followed by Ken Alford and various friends.

THE FIRST TRACTOR, c. 1944/5. The horses were replaced by a tractor towards the end of the war. Mr Ken Alford is behind the wheel in this picture taken in Pole Field, Exton.

THE AVENUE, EXTON, c. 1934, looking towards the main road. The cottage on the left is where Mr Pat Hardy ran the local post office for many years.

CHAPEL OF EASE, EXTON. This old cob-and-thatch chapel, which started its life as a barn, had been used for Church of England services for 100 years before it collapsed during a violent thunderstorm in 1960.

NUTWELL COURT stands about three and a half miles down the Exe from Topsham. It came to the Dinham family in the fourteenth century and was originally a small fort protecting the estuary on the side opposite Powderham. It played its part in both the Wars of the Roses and the Civil War and eventually came to the Drake family of Buckland. The house was much altered by a nephew, Lord Heathfield, in 1796, leaving just the chapel of the old building, visible on the right. The old road along the river to Exeter was then re-aligned outside the property.

GULLIFORD CHAPEL. In a once remote corner between Woodbury and Lympstone lies the old graveyard of Gulliford chapel, built after the Toleration Act of 1689, on land given by Thomas Lee of Sparkhayes, Gulliford and Ebford. It was supported by many prosperous local Dissenting families, including the Lees, the Smiths of Lympstone, the Barings of Exeter and the Stogdons of Woodbury Salterton, among others. The fine chapel was eventually erected in 1774. There was, however, a slow decline in attendance in the nineteenth century and finally the building was pulled down in 1907. The road past is still called Meeting Lane; it joins the A376 at Harefield Cross. This leads towards Woodbury, by Harefield (now St Peter's School), former home of the Peters family. Boundary Cottage to the right of the picture still remains.

PARSONAGE STILE HOUSE, once the home of Mr Worthington Brice, buried at Gulliford. He was a leading shipbuilder in the eighteenth century and traded in whale oil from an old jetty just above his house. It is said to have been a smuggling inn for a while, later still a dwelling, and was finally burnt down in the 1930s. This area is nowadays best observed from the train.

THE INLET AT PARSONAGE STILE, looking down towards the village, showing barrels of oil ready for loading, from a very old painting.

THE DARLING ROCK, from a water-colour of 1874, showing one of the stone boats which traded on the river until about 1910.

THE DARLING ROCK in the 1930s, looking across the estuary. By this time very little traffic was to be seen on the water.

CLIFF FIELD AND THE BOAT SHELTER, LYMPSTONE. Built in about 1860, when the railway came, the first shelter was destroyed by storms in 1897; the one shown here followed and was in turn rebuilt as it is today in 1936 by the men of the village.

MRS PETERS' TOWER, the most familiar building in Lympstone today, standing beside the Harefield Cottages built by Mr Peters in memory of his wife in 1885. You can also see one of the lime kilns, which, as has been seen earlier, existed all along this coast and were in use until the First World War. Notice also the many racks for drying the fishing nets, and, above, Highcliffe House, home of the Cox family.

QUAY LANE, LYMPSTONE, from a painting by H.B. Wimbush, looking across the river. It was painted in about 1900, before the Lord Roberts' Institute was made.

SOWDEN END and the southern edge of Lympstone. Called locally the mussel factory, after the First World War this enterprise marketed the varied and excellent shellfish of the river. In the photograph below men are seen putting the mussels into sacks. Gradually, however, the business became increasingly uneconomic and was closed. Its remains can be seen from the railway line between Lympstone and Exmouth.

VIEW TO THE GLOBE HOTEL, LYMPSTONE. When entering the village down what is still often called Cox's Hill, past Highcliffe House (and the many others now built on its land), the Globe Hotel is still a familiar landmark.

COX'S HILL, looking back up the road, with the Globe now on the left. On the right is the Lord Roberts' Institute (now the River House), opened in 1904 by Lord Roberts himself, a cousin of the Cox family. After the men returned from the Boer War, a need was felt for a more congenial meeting place, with a reading room, a billiards room and a rifle range, with facilities for plays and dancing. Early Women's Institute meetings took place in a large room downstairs.

THE CENTRE OF LOWER LYMPSTONE, with the Railway Inn (now the Swan) on the right – no car parking required then, but it was possible to hire cabs in the village. Mortimer's Stores are just visible on the left (now the Co-op). The bakery, until recently run by the same family, was above on the extreme left.

THE METHODIST SCHOOL ROOM AND CHAPEL. Down a private lane on the left of the last photograph, now the way to the car park, lie the Methodist schoolroom and chapel, shown here. The building was built in 1883, where once had been a boatyard.

MORTIMER'S STORES, the Lympstone emporium, which provided all the groceries, drapery and stationery, including many of the postcards of the village reproduced here. The railway, which had so altered life in Lympstone and Topsham, was just up the hill. Even at this time, around 1910, there were still twenty or thirty shops in a self-sufficient community, with shoemakers, dressmakers, and milliners, brewers and cidermakers, lace-makers, a working mill, bicycle shop, forge, saddler's and barber's.

LYMPSTONE STATION in its heyday, with a staff of at least five, a waiting-room (with a coal fire!), a ticket office and the side line which accommodated the freight trains serving the thirty or so working fishing boats, as well as delivering many incoming supplies.

THE LYMPSTONE BAND in the years soon after the First World War, when the men who had once been in the band of the Royal Devon Yeomanry Artillery had re-formed themselves. They are here seen escorting the Methodist Sunday school outing on their way up to Harefield, the Peters' house. Mrs Cox, in her familiar Bath chair, and Miss Cox watch their departure. It was some years before Sir Garbutt Nott of Courtlands presented the Lympstone Band with uniforms again.

THE PARISH CHURCH OF THE NATIVITY OF THE BLESSED VIRGIN MARY, LYMPSTONE, so dedicated in 1409 and unusual today. This rare photograph was taken before the restoration of the church in 1864.

HAYMAKING C. 1910. Opposite the church, in the big field belonging to the mill, in the centre of the old manor lands, half the villagers of Lympstone are at work.

UPPER LYMPSTONE and the main road to Exeter in about 1900. The Saddler's Arms and the then high wall of Bronte House are visible. The parish extends further, across the Woodbury – Budleigh road to Lympstone Common, which once provided grazing and the manorial rights for an independent village, something Lympstone has been since Saxon times.

SECTION FOUR
Public Services

CHRISTENING THE NEW FIRE-ENGINE, 1907. Provision was made for the 'accommodation of the parish fire-engine' by the Market House Trust in 1837. Here Mr Frank Luxton is leading the first horse across the quay for the first outing of the new engine on 24 August 1907. Below, the firemen in their smart uniforms are shown with the new engine. Mr Harry Gould is standing on the left. Second from the left is Mr Jack 'Cox' Bricknell, who was inseparable from his twin, Mr William 'Willow' Bricknell. Mr Henry Gould was the Officer in Charge of the Topsham Fire Service from 1907 to 1912 and he provided the two horses which pulled the engine.

OPENING OF THE TOPSHAM WATER WORKS, 1916. The gathering included members of St Thomas RDC and the Topsham Parish Council. Mr George Mortimore was the driver of the lorry which towed the fire-engine to the scene. The planks on the lorry were for the firemen to sit on when the engine was in tow. The water-tower was a circular tank with a capacity of 50,000 gallons. It was high enough to supply constant water to tanks in the roof of any house in the parish. The tower was taken down in 1984.

THE FIRST MOTOR FIRE-ENGINE AT CLYST ST GEORGE. A Morris tender towing a Morris trailer pump called *Aphrodite II* was bought in 1930 and was maintained by retained firemen. Mr Harry Gould raised the funds by public subscription.

DENNIS 'NEW WORLD BODY' FIRE-ENGINE with its team in front of Matthews Hall. The RDC took over the fire-fighting service in 1938 and provided this new engine in 1940. At that time Mr Sidney Mitchell was the First Officer and the drivers were Mr Bill Rowe and Mr Arthur Kennard. Mr Harry Gould is fourth from the left in the front row.

PUMP ON QUAY HILL, now Monmouth Hill. The name 'K. Pope, Topsham' is on the plaque fastened to the body of the pump. Pumping water up from the water-table provided Topsham's traditional water supply. Rainwater, filtered through local sandstone or river gravels, was relatively pure but could be contaminated.

RUSHMORE PUMPING STATION, between Newcourt and Exeter Road. Until 18 August 1916, when the new system was adopted, Topsham was almost entirely dependent on the 250 or so wells. The new pumping station and water-tower were officially opened on that date. The plaque above the entrance to the pumping station records that the building was erected by St Thomas Rural District Council. Mr Ern Hellier (on the left), standing in the doorway of the pumping station, was the engineer.

BRIDGE AND VIADUCT across the ship canal and River Exe at Topsham. In 1854 it was proposed that a line should branch off from the South Devon Railway, near Exminster, to be taken across the Exeter Canal and River Exe. This plan was never adopted; an artist's impression of this proposal is shown above. A branch of the London and South Western Railway was built to link Exeter and Exmouth and this line passes through Topsham.

TOPSHAM STATION before the First World War. The Exeter – Exmouth branch of the London and South Western Railway was opened in 1861. A long siding was taken down to the Quay, but its use was discontinued a century later, after the Beeching cuts, and the rails were lifted.

STATION BUILDING AND SIGNAL BOX, C. 1908. Both platforms were extended towards Exmouth at this time and, on the Exmouth side, the work appears to have been carried out by use of wooden sleepers. (As in the previous picture, the photographer has attracted considerable interest.)

MR JACK RICHARDS, SIGNALMAN, in Topsham signal box in the 1930s. Note the old-fashioned wall telephone with two ear-pieces and the hand tools neatly arranged near the gate-wheel.

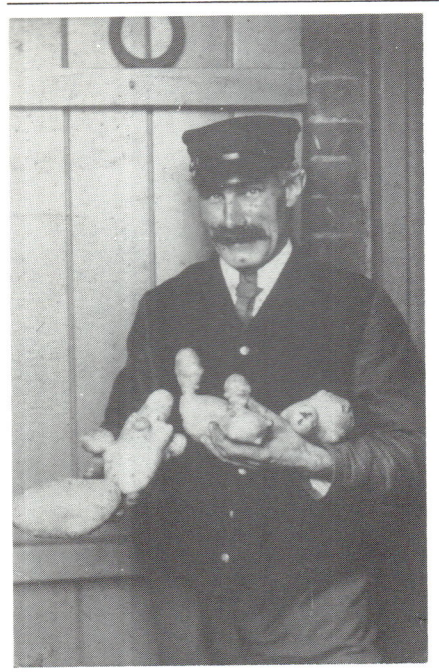

MR RICHARDS was a keen gardener who was very proud of his oddly-shaped potatoes.

PRIZE-WINNING LENGTH. In 1949 Mr R.A. Hamnett, Divisional Engineer, presented a cheque to ganger, Mr Peter Bater, and his team for the best-kept length of rail track. Shown are Inspector Pullen, Mr Frank Stone (sub-ganger), Mr W. Pope (patrolman), Mr Hamnett, Mr P. Bater (ganger), Mr E. Palmer (length-man), Mr Fred Tucker, Mr Johnny Fewings, Mr Bill Clark, Mr John Heard and Mr Bill Ford.

SECTION FIVE
Events and Social Life

TOPSHAM CORONATION DINNER.

SUBSCRIBER'S TICKET.

Admit *Major D'Urban & Lady*.

You are respectfully requested to join the Procession and co-operate with the General Committee in preserving order and harmony throughout the day, and to be provided with a plate, knife, fork and pint mug, for as many of your family as intend to Dine.

FORD, PRINTER, TOPSHAM.

A DINNER INVITATION to 'Major D'Urban and Lady' to celebrate the coronation of Queen Victoria. Instructions are given as to appropriate behaviour throughout the day. This invitation must have been addressed to William James D'Urban son of Sir Benjamin D'Urban (1777–1849). The town of Durban was named in his honour. His family home was at Newbard House, Topsham.

THE
TOPSHAM FANCY FAIR
For the BENEFIT of the
NATIONAL SCHOOLS
Established in that Town,
WILL BE HELD
On the Bowling-Green of the
SALUTATION-INN,
On Thursday *the* 8th *of* August.

It is hoped every person will contribute, at the entrance, not less than a Shilling, for the Benefit of the Institution.

The FAIR will open at 12 o'Clock.

It is requested that all Donations of Fancy Work may be forwarded to the Rev. H. Thoap, Treasurer to the Schools, on or before Saturday the 3rd of August.

Contributions of Confectionary, Fruit, Plants, Flowers, &c. will be particularly acceptable and may be forwarded to the Treasurer the day preceding the Fair.

Dated Topsham, July 19th, 1833.

A POSTER from 1833 advertising Topsham Fancy Fair for the benefit of the National schools sponsored by the Church of England. (Photographs courtesy of Mrs G.D. Borradaile.)

HESTER FROOD (1882–1971), a daughter of Dr James Frood, who returned with his family from New Zealand in 1889 to live at Broadway House, High Street, in Topsham. Hester later studied at an atelier in Paris and her work, both water-colours and etchings, is now being appreciated nationally as that of a significant woman artist.

MAX HOLMAN in his sailor suit.

A PENNY-FARTHING BICYCLE. Miss Dorothy Holman remembered her uncles riding this particular cycle at Grove House. It is now in Topsham Museum.

TOPSHAM CYCLE CLUB IN THE GROUNDS OF THE RETREAT. Sir Alexander Hamilton is in the centre (in slouch hat). Others include Mr Ern Hellier, Mr Ted Chestnut, Mr Dickie Hooper and Mr Burrows (Sir Alexander's coachman). Cycles were very simple before the First World War, with wooden rims and neither gears nor brakes.

MR HARRY GOULD'S FIRST MOTOR CYCLE, c. 1900, outside St Nicholas' Methodist church. The wall behind Mr Gould was demolished before 1908 to allow for the building of the Memorial Hall. Mr Gould was an active and public-spirited man involved in many activities, including the fire service. He also set up the town's first cinema.

HORSE-DRAWN OPEN WAGONETTE in Fore Street, Topsham, c. 1900, preparing for an outing.

A HORSE-DRAWN COVERED WAGONETTE with curtains and carriage-lamp. This photograph dates from before 1914. Eastmans Ltd, the butcher's shop, then occupying part of Cromer House, closed down shortly after this event.

A CHARABANC OUTING, outside Broadway House, High Street. Mr and Mrs G. Autton are at the back of the vehicle with their son. The driver is Mr Harry Gould.

A SPORTS CAR for the younger generation at Pytte House.

A PRESENTATION AT COURT, before the First World War. Miss Dorothy Holman (on the left) with her mother, Mrs Herbert Holman, and her sister, Miss Joyce Holman. Miss Dorothy Holman's dress and train are made of cream silk satin. The low-necked bodice and short net sleeves are trimmed with bugle bead embroidery. The high waist is emphasized by a decoration of padded crescents stitched with silver and cream thread. Mrs Holman's dress is made of grey satin trimmed with gold. The train is grey velvet lined with gold silk. (The photograph is reproduced by kind permission of the Exeter Museums Service. Miss D. Holman's gown is at Rougemont House Museum, Exeter.)

A CHILDREN'S PARTY AT FOLLETT LODGE, 1894. Among those present were Mr Richard Holman (in a top hat).

A GARDEN PARTY AT GROVE HOUSE in June 1924.

A PICNIC AT THE WARREN, 1894. Members of the Holman family and friends.

THE RECREATION GROUND, donated by Mr Herbert Holman to the town in the 1920s. The Recreation Ground (once a timber pound) was built up from waste collected by the dustman with his horse and cart. About once a year there would be 'rat week' when the fire brigade would flood out the rats, which would then be killed!

THE *CECILY*. Miss Cecily Goodman (left) with friends on board the *Cecily* in 1907. The vessel was probably named in her honour by her father, a dentist, who was a keen sailor. Miss Goodman was one of a team of six women bell-ringers who rang the bells at the parish church for forty-three years, until her retirement at the age of seventy. According to a printed notice on bell-ringing donated to the museum by Miss Pamela Collings, 'The first time these bells were rung by LADY RINGERS was Easter Day, March 31st, 1918 at 6 a.m. for Early Celebration.'

JUBILEE PIER. Mr 'Chuggy' Amos lived at the Elms on the Strand in the early 1900s. Members of his family are here sitting on the Jubilee Pier. The two boys are Arthur and Maurice Amos. The pier was built in 1887 to mark the Golden Jubilee of Queen Victoria. It was dismantled in 1921 after a young boy, Tom Pym, was sadly drowned after falling through some rotting boards.

MEMBERS OF THE 'BEER AND BACCY BAND' shown in an early photography.

IN LATER LIFE Mr J. Bricknell, Mr E.A. Sandford and Mr W. Bricknell still wear their uniform with pride. (Messrs J. and W. Bricknell were twins. See page 128.)

TOPSHAM LOCAL BAND in 1913. The bandsmen and the instruments may be the same but the uniform is smarter. The peaked caps with the white cap-covers could be seen today.

TOPSHAM SILVER BAND leading the carnival procession at Hannaford's Quay, followed by the fire-engine. The carnival used to assemble in front of the premises of Carr & Quicke, cider-makers, (formerly the Dry Dock) in the Strand. Topsham Silver Band started in 1888 as the 'Beer and Baccy' Band. Three of the original members were Mr J. Bricknell, Mr William Bricknell and Mr E.A. Sandford. Later it became the 'Topsham Band' and, after the Second World War, it was called the 'Topsham Silver Band'. The band amalgamated with Lympstone Band in 1960.

SMOKE
LLOYD'S-EXETER
BROADARE AND TOPSHAM MIXTURE

WHICH WERE THE FIRST TOBACCOS

THE DEVONS HAD TO SMOKE

AFTER THEIR LONG SIEGE

IN LADYSMITH.

GOOD OLD SMOKES!   CANNOT BE BEATEN!

AN ADVERTISEMENT FROM EARLY THIS CENTURY, referring to the Devons' involvement in the siege of Ladysmith, in the Boer War.

ALLAHABAD, INDIA, 1915. Exeter and Topsham men of the 1st Devon Battery, 4th Wessex Brigade Territorials. Pte. Frank Davey, whose father was lock-keeper at Turf from 1910 to 1918, sits on the left behind the man with the signalling flag. The son of Capt. Collings of Victoria Cottage, Topsham, is also in the photograph.

FIRST RIFLE VOLUNTEERS. Men from Topsham and Clyst St George in the playground of the Topsham Boys' School (now Topsham Middle School). Major Harry Gould is seated in the centre of the front row.

FIRST RIFLE VOLUNTEERS at camp, 1914.

STAFF AND PATIENTS AT THE VOLUNTARY AID HOSPITAL during the First World War. Standing, left to right: Nurse Eliza Chambers, Pte. Horrocks, Farrier Sergeant Hiscock, Nurse Cookson, Ptes. Harris, Cohen, King, Stumbles, Gunner Sullivan, Nurse Glanville. Seated: Nurse Thomas, Nurse Symons, the Matron, Mr F. Young, Nurse Fulford, and possibly Mrs Ashford. The photograph was taken in the garden of Riversmeet House, Elm Grove Road.

LACE-MAKING AT SCHOOL in the 1930s. Mrs Elsie Luxton MBE, as a girl, sitting in the back row on the right, learned to make lace at school in Honiton Clyst. Mrs Luxton, who has made her home in Topsham, has become an expert in Honiton lace-making and she is carrying on an old-established tradition in the town. Many people remember Mrs Bess Hussey and Mrs Eliza Luxon with their pillows making lace on Hannaford's Quay in the early 1900s.

STAFF OUTING FOR MR HARRY GOULD'S BUILDING FIRM in the 1920s. This firm built the Matthews Hall in 1927. Mr Clifford Gould can be seen standing in the back row, second right; Mr Gould was later the Topsham postmaster.

TOPSHAM BOWLING CLUB, c. 1930. The club was founded in 1928 and its first president was Mr Woodrow Matthews. Mr T. Pott (front row, second left) was the first captain.

TOPSHAM FOOTBALL CLUB was formed in 1908 as Topsham St Margaret's. The club played at the Bowling-Green Marshes until 1953. Mr Sidney Baker writes that he was sorry to see St Margaret's had been dropped from the name of the Topsham football team because as Topsham St Margaret's they were known and feared all over Devon. Among the team pictured below are Mr Reg Luscombe (centre), the Revd Arthur Rich (front row, second left) and the famous Mr Dick 'Pincher' Pym (front row, fourth left; see also p. 51), who played in three Cup Finals and was president of Topsham Football Club until his death in 1988.

SAILING PAST THE CHURCH. The sheds in front of the later Church House belonged to the Wigzells firm, which closed down in 1865.

PASSING THE CLUBHOUSE. The 'B' class fleet with *Marguerita* in the foreground, sailed by Mr Fred Litton and his daughter, Doris, passing the clubhouse on Hawkins Quay in the mid-1930s. Topsham Sailing Club was founded in 1885 and used a wooden clubhouse at Langdale Wharf until 1919 when the club moved to Hawkins Quay. The land there was bought outright in 1941.

SOME OF TOPSHAM HOME GUARD photographed outside the tennis pavilion, Red Rock. Front row, left to right: Messrs Abraham Edworthy, Gerry Copland, Wally Paine, Tom Ley, Jack Richards, Billy Ingham, Reg Luscombe and Charlie Lucy. Back row: Messrs Bert Kentisbeer, Jack Nethercott, M. Powley, Cecil 'Tacker' Rowe, Jim Norton, P. Alexander, Sid Collins and Bert May.

AFTER THE BOMBING. Clyst St George church was destroyed by enemy action on 31 August 1940. An incendiary bomb which fell directly on to the organ set the whole church on fire. The tower and walls, though damaged, were the only part not destroyed. The church of Clyst St George was the first to be destroyed by enemy action during the Second World War. Mr John Pym was the choirboy on the left and the rector, the Revd Armstrong, is on the right.

GAS MASKS IN USE AT CLYST ST GEORGE SCHOOL.

PILOTS' SIGNATURES AT THE GEORGE AND DRAGON, CLYST ST GEORGE. During the war many pilots who flew from Exeter Airport were billeted at the George and Dragon in Clyst St George. It became a tradition for them to sign their names on the bar ceiling. Mr Bill Moor, the publican from 1946 to 1973, is seen here inspecting the autographs, which include those of a number of Battle of Britain pilots.

VICTORY CELEBRATION held at Pynes' Barn in 1945.

THE LAST MARCH OF THE TOPSHAM BRANCH OF THE BRITISH LEGION.

THE FURRY DANCE IN TOPSHAM in the late 1940s. Members of the Topsham Youth Club, wearing the 'new look', are seen dancing in Fore Street. Miss Dorothy Holman set up the youth club in 1940 using the sail loft behind her home at 25 the Strand (now Topsham Museum) as the meeting place.

TOPSHAM SENIOR CITIZENS' CHOIR in 1956 – a happy and confident group.

TOPSHAM'S FIRST MUSEUM. A photograph of an oil painting of F.W.L. Ross, a noted ornithologist, by local artist, James Leakey (1775–1865). The artist's son was the Revd John Arundell Leakey, who was vicar of St Margaret's church, Topsham, from 1857 to 1880. The painting was bought by the Royal Albert Memorial Museum, Exeter, in 1895. Mr Ross built a gallery at Broadway House in Topsham, where he lived, to house his specimens of stuffed birds, including many aquatic British birds, collected on the Exe estuary. After his death his widow donated his collection to the new Royal Albert Memorial Museum in 1866.

BOYS BRIGADE. The late Mr Bryan Baker, here aged nine, as a 'lifebuoy' with his brother, Alan, aged twelve, standing outside the Methodist church with Mr Black, who was in charge of the local brigade. Bryan Baker was to become the Founder Member and Chairman from 1969 to 1979 of the Topsham Birdwatching and Naturalist Society. Bryan's love of wildlife and of the estuary endeared him to all who knew him.

AN OPEN-AIR PERFORMANCE in 1951 of an excerpt from *A Midsummer Night's Dream* by members of the Topsham Amateur Dramatic Society, produced by Mair Staniland in Miss Dorothy Holman's garden. The Dramatic Society was formed in 1928, just after the Matthews Hall was built (see page 65). Their first production was *Tilley from Bloomsbury*.

MISS DOROTHY HOLMAN'S MUSEUM. Miss Holman is shown here in part of the sail loft where she established her museum in 1967. Iron rings are still fixed to the walls. Miss Holman looked after the museum until her death in 1983. The museum was re-opened, to include the whole of the premises at No. 25 the Strand, in 1986.

ACKNOWLEDGEMENTS

However hard one tries it would be quite impossible to thank adequately all those who have contributed valuable information as material for this book. Many people, particularly members of the Topsham Museum Society, have spoken from their own personal knowledge of times past and their acquaintance with the characters who have figures in the events which are depicted.

The two main sources of photographs are the Dorothy Holman collection and the Morice Parsons collection. Topsham Museum Society re-established the museum in 1986 and inherited from the founder, Miss Dorothy Holman, a priceless collection of photographs of members of the Holman family and the ships that they built. From this collection we have drawn many of the photographs shown, including prints from nineteenth-century daguerrotypes and cabinet portraits. Councillor Morice Parsons has, over the years, built up an extensive collection of more recent photographs which he kindly donated to the museum in 1989. These have also been a most valuable pictorial record.

Groups of photographs of a specialized nature have been loaned by Mrs J. Browne, Miss E. Gibbs, Mr and Mrs L. Gould and Mr and Mrs J. Bowden. Individual people who kindly loaned us photographs or helped in some way include: The Alford family • Lady Alment • Mr Amos • Mrs M. Arbuary • Mr D. Axford • Mr and Mrs H.C. Baker • Mr M. Benn • Mrs G.D. Borradaile • Mrs U. Brighouse • Mrs Brimblecombe • Mr and Mrs N. Cheffers • Mr N. Cheffers-Heard • Mr K. Dean • Mr E. Delderfield • Mrs J. Duckworth • Mrs Edworthy • Miss S. Follett • Mrs G. Gullidge • Mr P. Hardy • Mr Hayward and the Lady Seward School • Miss A. Hellier • Mr Bob Irish • Mrs M. Kirkman • Mr B. Lane of Topsham Middle School • Revd D.H. Large • Mr Dick May • Mr I. Merry • Mr and Mrs W. Moor • Mr and Mrs W. Nott • Mrs F. Owen • Mrs A. Price • Mr G. Pridmore • Mr I. Putnam • Mr R. Ridding • Mrs N. Steven • Topsham Sailing Club • Topsham WI • Mr Daniel Trout • Mr E. Voysey • Mr J. Voysey • Mr Roy Wheeler and Mr and Mrs W. Wills.

Details of the source of any of the material used in this book may be obtained from the Topsham Museum Society.